How to Book of Interpersonal Communication: Improve Your Relationships

interpersonal skills, assertion skills at work, dealing with conflict, interpersonal relationships

Author
J H Hood

ISBN
978-0-9875575-5-1

Copyright
Copyright 2013 J H Hood

Dedication

To all those people who have and are still walking the learning journey with me—thank you a thousand times over.
May we continue the journey with joy in the challenges.

Published by WordCraft Global Pty Ltd

Contents

The journey 5
Key Principles 7
Checklists 9
Changing Habits: Setting Goals 10
The basics of good communication 13
Body Language 15
    Virtual Body Language 17
Knowing yourself: ways of being aware 19
The Johari Window 21
Visual Auditory & Kinesthetic (VAK) 23
    VAK and Virtual Communication 27
Assertion skills 29
    Aggressive Behavior 30
    Passive Behavior 32
    Passive–Aggressive Behavior 34
    Assertive Behavior 36
Assertiveness techniques 38
Active Listening 42
Questioning techniques 46
Some More Techniques for Dealing with Difficult Communication Situations 47
The World of Virtual Interpersonal Communication 52
Collaborative problem resolution 56
Conclusion 58

Some useful references 59
Checklist 1—Changing habits: Setting Goals 60
   An Example of a Plan 61
Checklist 2—Planning your Communication 64
Checklist 3— Visual Auditory Kinesthetic 66
Checklist 4—Practicing Assertion 68
Checklist 5—Understanding your audience 70
Checklist 6—Disagreements, differences and conflict 72
Disclaimer 73
Author Profile 74

The journey

"Knowing others is intelligence, knowing yourself is wisdom"
           Chinese proverb

Welcome to this stage of your life long journey of:
- **improving** your self esteem
- **increasing** your communication skills
- **building** wonderful interpersonal relationships
- dealing **positively** with the complexities of our world
- **reducing** your stress levels

On this journey, you will explore:
- **principles** for communicating well
- understanding yourself—**your preferences** for communicating
- understanding **others**
- communicating **assertively**

As you work your way through this how to book, you will know yourself better, and widen your understanding of others—**at home, at work and at play.**

The better our communication skills, the better our lives—as individuals, as communities and as nations. The wonderful thing is that we can **all** learn to become better communicators—in fact, good communicators **never stop learning.**

We are all born with the **'fight or flight'** response. If we feel threatened, our instincts tell us to stay and fight, or to run for safety. The difficulty is that in most of the situations we find ourselves in nowadays, these two responses rarely get us the best outcomes. And often we get stuck in a round of fight or aggressive communication and flight or passive communication.

One of the big secrets to improving our relationships is to get out of that pattern. To understand yourself, to learn how to **pause** before reacting emotionally— and consequently to give yourself **a wider range** of options in the way you relate with people.

As we broaden our range of communications options we can then better understand—and deal with—the consequences of the options we choose.

We now understand that there is another option that we can learn—that of **assertive communication**—that with practice, brings exceptional rewards. This skill you will learn here!

It is one of the best ways to improve all your relationships.

Key Principles

"Every fight is one between different angles of vision illuminating the same truth."
                Mahatma Gandhi

Good communicators understand that:
- most people have a reason for their behavior—**which makes sense to them**. You may not see why, but for them it is the best thing—for who they are at that moment
- disagreement or conflict that is **not addressed doesn't go away**
- disagreement or conflict addressed **early** is often easier to resolve
- if what we want is not happening, then we need to **try something different**—to stop doing the same thing over and over again
- what we **do** and what we **are** are two different things—we need to separate the behavior from the person. We are all more than the behavior we produce— and we can all learn to change our behavior

A key component of improving all your interpersonal relationships is to understand yourself: **what makes you tick—and react!** We

need to be self aware, to understand **how we manage ourselves**. This means:
- being aware of our **own feelings** and how our feelings affect our behavior
- knowing **our strengths and limits** -- knowing when to ask for help
- building our levels of **self-respect** and good self-esteem
- being able to **keep disruptive emotions under control**
- understanding the degree to which we can be **honest** and trustworthy
- being able to see the **positive** in what is happening, building resilience

As well, it is important to understand how we **manage relationships**. How we:
- have **empathy** with others—our skills in understanding others' perspectives and taking an interest in their concerns
- use social skills—our effectiveness in **encouraging the responses** we want in others

It is okay to avoid people who invalidate you. While this is not always possible, at least try to spend less time with them, or to not give them psychological power over you.

Mutual respect is at the centre of all good communication

Checklists

There are **Checklists** included at the end of this how to book.

Many people find that Checklists are a good way of keeping the learning going, and a way of making sure that the ideas and techniques stay in your mind.

The **Checklists** are designed to be used in a range of ways:
- when working on your personal communication goals—especially assertiveness
- when looking for options and different ways of communicating with others—in all spheres of your life
- for understanding the communication preferences of the people around you
- to help manage conflict, and to better understand other people's behavior

Checklist 1—Changing Habits

Checklist 2—Planning Your Communication

Checklist 3—Visual, Auditory and Kinesthetic

Checklist 4—Practicing Assertion

Checklist 5—Understanding Your Audience

Checklist 6—Disagreements, Differences and Conflict

Changing Habits: Setting Goals

*'habit....tendency to act in a certain way,
especially by frequent repetition of the same act'*
Oxford English Dictionary

*If something is not working, then don't do more of the same...
...do something different.*

Be prepared to change!

We communicate all the time—it is as automatic and as important as breathing.

While our intentions are to connect successfully with others, no matter how much effort we put in, we experience mis–communication, poor communication, unexpected conflict and people who seem to deliberately work at being difficult.

We interact with others using learned patterns... unthinking reactions...**habits** that we have developed from our life experiences.

Time and again:
- we get locked into **patterns** and routines
- **new situations and people** unsettle our ways of communicating

- **differences in expectations** between people—and between generations—cause barriers

It is no good continuing to do more of the same—*if you want different and better interactions with others, then you must change some of the things you do now!*

One of the key blockages when we want to improve the ways in which we relate to people is that **habits can be tough to change!**

An action or behavior takes **28 days of repetition** to become a habit.

You can increase your success rate in changing habits by:
- having a **plan**—they say *"if you fail to plan, you plan to fail"*—think about it!
- using small, clear **goals** that are realistic and achievable
- setting yourself realistic **time frames**
- accepting that **you will make some mistakes** and not succeed every time—this is natural, and a good way to learn
- being **persistent**
- **not doing it all by yourself.** Get some support—friends, your partner, family, colleagues, or someone you feel you can trust

Make your goals SMART:
- Specific—clearly defined
- Measurable—know that you have arrived

- Achievable—within reach
- Relevant—practical
- Time bound—set a time limit to work towards

Here are some other hints to use when writing your goals. Make them:
- **SMALL**—make them manageable, both in terms of time and what you are going to do
- **SPECIFIC**—goals need to be definite and detailed, something you can see yourself doing
- **REASONABLE**—each goal should make sense, you should be able to see the value in doing it
- **POSITIVE**—decide what you will do rather than what you will not do
- **REPETITIOUS**—choose goal behavior you will be able to work at often
- **INDEPENDENT**—try to set goals that are not dependent on the behavior of others

Take some time now to identify some specific areas that you want to enhance or improve, and then use **Checklist 1** to start you on your voyage. Don't set yourself up to fail—start small and make your goals Achievable!

It may help you to think of **Checklist 1** as the itinerary or map of this stage of your communication journey.

Want to do something different? Use: **Checklist 1—Changing Habits**

The basics of good communication

DON'T MAKE ASSUMPTIONS
"Find the courage to ask questions and to express what you really want. Communicate with others as clearly as you can to avoid misunderstandings, sadness, and drama."
          'The Four Agreements' Don Miguel Ruiz

Simplicity is the key to good communication.

Good communicators share information in a clear and straightforward way, they give constructive feedback and accept differences in style.

Poor communicators are more likely to keep information to themselves, to give unclear or confusing messages, to criticize rather than to give useful feedback.

Plan your Communication—try asking these questions:
- **why** are you communicating?
- who is your **audience**?
- **how** will you communicate?
- how will you get **feedback**?

As you think about your communication, ask yourself:
- **what** is it that you want to achieve?
- **who** needs to know?
- **what** do you want someone to do—or know—as a result of this communication?

Being an effective communicator is a two-way process—and the real communication is the message that is actually received, not necessarily the message you intended.

What we say is not always what is heard and understood.

We all **filter messages** through our own perceptions, contexts and needs, and these affect the ways in which we send and receive all communication.

In this increasingly global village, we need to understand the **filters of different cultures, customs, rules and social behavior.**

For example:
- in some cultures, if you don't look someone straight in the eye, then you are considered to be untrustworthy; while in others, it is considered courteous to look down as someone speaks to you
- how we use *yes* and *no*: '*Were you or were you not present at the time*' Answer '*Yes*' :meaning I was not present at the time, or '*No*': meaning I was present at the time

You can take this filtering into account by developing your skills in:
- listening and clarifying: try asking questions
- anticipating problems and difficulties
- understanding the other person—sharing perceptions and needs: try sharing experiences

- keeping your message simple—less opportunity for misunderstanding or misinterpretation
- setting up ways of getting open feedback

Body Language

The way the message is delivered is as important as the words.

How you communicate is as important as **what** you communicate.

In **face to face** communication—including telephone conversations—generally people:
- take only about 10% of the meaning from the **words** that are used
- 50% is read from **body** language
- the remaining 30% to 40% comes from the **tone of voice**

Only a very small percentage of the message is actually conveyed by words—the voice tone, volume, rate of speech, facial non-verbal messages and body postures communicate **the major portion** of the message. This **body language** is the unspoken message that your body is sending.

In face to face communication, people will usually believe what the body language, or non verbal component, of the message is saying.

An example is when some one says '*Yes I understand*' in a hesitant voice and with a puzzled facial expression—you will believe the *non verbal* language, and realize that they probably *don't* understand.

Consider your own **body language**.

What are you communicating about yourself in:
- the way you dress
- the way you stand—your posture?
- your facial expressions?
- the tone of your voice?

Are you happy with what you are communicating? What might you think of changing? Why?

What about the people around you? What is their body language telling you?

Everyone sends out non verbal cues. It is important to be aware of your own and other people's body language and to develop your **observation skills**.

Use your **eyes as well as your ears** to listen, see and understand what is being communicated.

Check the context—if a person has folded their arms—often an indication of annoyance—it may simply be that the person is cold. So, you will make more accurate interpretations if you **look for clusters of actions**. If the person has folded their arms, and is <u>**also**</u> avoiding eye contact <u>**and**</u> speaking in flat tone of voice, then it is highly likely that they *are* annoyed.

Good communicators are sensitive to changes in behavior. With people we know, we can improve our communication if we notice changes in behavior—observing the clues that alert us to the need to clarify and question.

We also **interpret patterns of behavior**—particularly where we know people well enough to recognize that they regularly react in certain ways. If we know, from past experience, that someone cries when they are happy—or laughs when they are embarrassed— we deal differently with them than with someone we may be meeting for the first time.

Improve your skills in dealing with non verbal communication by:
- **listening actively:** we *talk* at about 100-120 words per minute, but we *think* at about 400-500 words per minute—keep your attention on **what** is being said and **how** it is being said
- **observing** what is happening—look for context, clusters, changes in behavior
- asking clarifying questions

Virtual Body Language

Now, many of us choose to **communicate virtually**—via SMS, Twitter, email, FaceBook, chat rooms and other social networking tools.

This brings another complexity to good interpersonal communication as most of **the meaning** that body language gives to both face to face and telephone communication **is absent**.

We consider virtual interpersonal communication in more detail later in this book. At this point, it is important to think about **how the lack of body language cues may affect your communication choices**.

Use Checklist 2 as a guide to planning your communication.

Knowing yourself: ways of being aware

"Know yourself"
   The god Apollo, from Greek mythology

Knowing yourself is about learning to better understand why you feel what you feel and why you behave in a particular way. Once you begin to understand this, **then you can add other techniques to your skills toolbox and change the tools that are not of best use to you.** You can improve your life and happiness.

Some words of caution about using these tools—especially the descriptions of preferences and behavior patterns:

1. *As with all generalizations, there are always exceptions*
2. *As we grow and learn, our range of options within our preferences also widen*

3. ***These descriptions are tools for understanding, not boxes to put people in!***
4. ***There are no 'right' or 'wrong' answers—each preference is valid in its own right—their usefulness is in how we can use them to understand ourselves and others***

Most people have a reason for their behavior—which makes sense to them. Good communicators work to understand their own preferences and those of others, and are able to adapt their interactions to work with them.

We all have **different ways** of how we prefer to relate to—and behave in—the world. These may be from our genes, our families and our cultures, as well as those learned through our personal experiences.

These preferences affect the ways we communicate and the ways in which we understand others.

When we communicate, we speak—or write or act—from **our own experiences and with our own preferences**. Other people interpret those words based on **their own** experiences, preferences and meaning.

We are all different, yet, fortunately:
- there are some **common patterns** in how we behave
- there are an **interesting and varied range of ways** of describing patterns and preferences in behavior
- **learning to understand ourselves and others** increases our chances of communicating more effectively

Over the next sections you will find a range of tools that you can use to improve your understanding of yourself and how you communicate, as well as improving your understanding of the people around you.

The Johari Window

The Johari window is a tool developed by psychologists Joseph Luft and Harry Ingham in the 1950's, called the 'Johari' window when they combined their first names—Joe and Harry. It has kept its relevance over the years.

It is a tool for improving self awareness, as well as understanding how others see us. It uses two concepts:
- we can **build trust** with others by telling them information about ourselves
- we can **learn more about ourselves** by asking others about how they experience us

Here is a diagram of the **Johari Window**

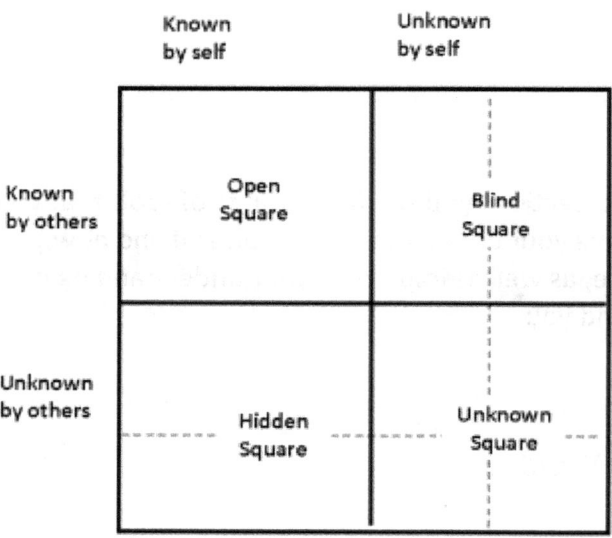

You can see that there are four squares:

The **open** square—what you know about yourself, and what others also know about you: skills, some of what motivates you, behavior patterns, knowledge and so on.

The **blind** square—what you don't know about yourself, but others know about you: behaviors and reactions which others observe but you may not realize you are doing, and so on.

The **hidden** square—what you know about yourself, but others don't know: some preferences, some of the things that motivate you, some feelings, and so on.

The **unknown** square—what is unknown both to you and to others: skills or interests that you haven't yet tried out or thought about, things that new experiences or feedback can identify.

The aim of using the Johari window is to **increase the Open Square**, and **decrease the Unknown Square.** You can see this demonstrated by the dotted line in the diagram above.

As you give information and receive feedback, you can see how the **sizes of the squares change**—the dotted line in the diagram. And so we continue to understand more about ourselves and the people we are close to, get better at expressing ourselves and relate better to others.

There are two things to **be careful** about when sharing information:
- be **sensible about what you disclose to others**—very personal things may be fine with a close friend, but quite inappropriate with a colleague at work
- be **sensitive when giving feedback**—be aware of cultural issues or the other person's state of mind and confidence

Use **Active Listening** skills—described a bit further in this book—and use empathy.

Visual Auditory & Kinesthetic (VAK)

The earth is a beehive; we all enter by the same door but live in different cells
Bantu proverb

You can't see the whole sky through a bamboo tube
Japanese proverb

A good starting point is to understand our preferences in the way we receive, code, store and give meaning to our experiences. They are the ways by which we prefer to receive external information and process it internally.

The three most common styles are: **visual, auditory or kinesthetic**. We all tend to use one style about 70% of the time.

A person with a **visual** preference speaks and processes information through visual pathways—sight—and tends to:
- have images of their experiences
- like to see or write down instructions or new information
- prefer to interact with others in person—like to see what the other person's reactions are
- remember information better if they write it down
- want to be shown concepts or ideas
- remember faces more easily than names
- use words such as *'see, picture, look, light, show, appears...'*
- may dislike background noise or music

A visual person will tend to prefer visual information: written instructions, charts, graphs, letters and memos, films and videos and prefers to provide written reports.

A person with an **auditory** preference speaks and processes information through auditory pathways—sound—and tends to:
- enjoy discussions and prefers to hear instructions or new information

- prefer to learn by listening and asking questions
- need to ask questions as they listen—and not be silent until the other person has finished speaking
- not follow written instructions well
- want to talk about their experiences
- talk through issues and finds it useful to have someone who they can talk their ideas through with
- be more responsive to the tone of someone's voice
- use words like *'hear, say, listen, talk, sounds, voice, orchestrate, in tune with...'*

An auditory person prefers conversations, discussions and phone calls, and prefers to explain what they've done, or ask for verbal feedback.

A person with a **kinesthetic** preference speaks and processes information through feeling pathways, experiences sensations and may have feelings about them, and tends to:
- rarely read the instructions or directions first—they solve problems using trial and error
- draw on their feelings to make decisions
- learn by doing and moving—can lose concentration if there is little external stimulation or movement
- like demonstrations and actual physical samples
- not be good at giving step by step instructions
- use words such as *'feel, handle, relaxed, grasp, change, concrete, up against...'*
- respond to physical rewards and touching

A kinesthetic person prefers demonstrations and real examples, and prefers tasks which require movement and a chance to identify how they feel about a situation.

So—which is your preferred style? Which of the three descriptions is most like you—is your preference visual, auditory or kinesthetic?

Remember that we all use all of the channels at some times, but we do generally prefer to use one channel. We respond best to, and through, that channel.

How can understanding your preference, and that of others, help in the way you communicate?

Consider the way we **give and receive directions**. Quite simply, you will respond better yourself, and get better results, if you **match VAK** styles. For example:

- draw a map for a visual person to follow
- give an auditory person verbal instructions, while giving them an opportunity to ask questions
- give the kinesthetic person a copy of the map, and let them draw the route on it

If you **have a message** for someone, consider:

- a written note for a visual person
- a phone call for an auditory person
- talking in person to a kinesthetic person

Think back on some of the reactions that you may have had, or seen, **when talking with someone**. It is highly likely that the communication in each of the following situations was less than effective because there was:

- a lack of eye contact with a visual person
- no opportunity to speak from the other person in an interaction with an auditory person
- no emotional response or support from the other person in an interaction with a kinesthetic person

If you can match your communication with the thinking style of others, you are more likely to communicate effectively.

You will significantly improve your communication skills if you practice:

- listening to others and identifying their preferred channels
- matching their channels in the words you use and the means by which you communicate

Note: This VAK way of describing the way we receive and structure information is part of the theory of **Neuro Linguistic Programming—NLP**. There are many other aspects to discover as you read and explore the topic further—especially on the Internet.

VAK and Virtual Communication

You will remember: we said that most people use one preference about 70% of the time. This means that for people whose primary channels are either auditory or kinesthetic, the **visual nature of most virtual communication may pose issues.**

When you choose virtual communication means, you need to be prepared to:
- think about whether this particular message should be face to face
- provide opportunities for people to ask questions
- consider your own preferences—for example, are you a kinesthetic who isn't very good at giving instructions? How can you improve that a virtual environment?
- consider how formal or informal you need to be in this communication. If it is very formal, use hard copy
- be careful when writing or responding emotionally. We tend to lose the emotional filters we apply in face to face communication as soon as we go virtual! And unfortunately this can lead to some very awkward and painful interactions

Use **Checklist 3—Visual, Auditory & Kinesthetic** to use VAK to improve your interactions.

Add practice in understanding and matching VAK preferences to your goals in **Checklist 1 'Changing Habits'**.

Assertion skills

Know what's going on
'The Universal Heart' Stephanie Dowrick

We are all born with the **'Fight or Flight'** response. When faced with danger our **instincts** tell us to stay and fight, or to run for safety.

These are very natural behaviors, and have their place in our communication skills repertoire—but, if they are **our usual or only ways of communicating,** then over time they can become very destructive in all our relationships.

We can often get caught in a **cycle of passive and aggressive behavior,** swinging from one extreme to the other. However, by learning to recognize when you are experiencing—or using—aggressive and passive behavior, and practicing **assertive behavior,** you will increase your range of options and improve your outcomes when communicating.

We all tend to swing between three ways of communicating:
- **aggressive** behavior—**fight** response
- **passive** behavior—**flight** response
- **assertive** behavior—responses based on **mutual respect**

Some of us also can be caught in a cycle of **passive–aggressive** behavior, where our actions are passive but our feelings are aggressive.

Not surprisingly, of the three, **assertive behavior** is the most effective, and one which we can all learn to use. Assertive communication:
- improves self-confidence
- leads to honest relationships
- encourages the resolution of issues, more quickly and painlessly
- leads to less gossip
- keeps negotiations open
- enables mutual respect

While assertive communication skills do take some courage as you practice—it is LESS STRESSFUL overall!!!!

The first step is to learn to recognize when we—or others—are using each of the three behaviors. There are examples of each in the following tables.

Aggressive Behavior

AGGRESSIVE BEHAVIOR: When people are being aggressive, they:	You will usually observe:
• express feelings	• an abrupt, firm, loud voice

and opinions in a way which punishes, threatens or puts the other person down • usually leave the other person with the bad feeling that they have lost—and sets up a poor environment for future transactions • can be seen as bullying • are manipulative • are about making sure that they get what they want, no matter what the other person feels	• demanding and dominating behavior i.e. talk over people, insist on their own opinion, twist what the other says to suit themselves • bullying • criticism, blame, calling people names, making threats, offering unasked for advice • not allowing others to communicate their thoughts, feelings, desires and needs • invading personal space • not being prepared to discuss facts or to change their position on anything • confrontation in a destructive way • making all the decisions, everyone else has no choice—'I win, you lose'

Aggressive communication often ignores the impact of one's behavior on others. It is an "**I win, you lose**" position. Aggressive behavior includes many forms of domination and direct manipulation. Aggression usually aims at getting control of situations or getting one's goals met no matter what the consequences are to others.

Aggressive behavior can be:
- judging

- criticizing
- out-talking, out-reasoning, out-lasting
- being louder or more threatening
- using money, status, physical attributes, attractiveness, or other resources to get control

Passive Behavior

PASSIVE BEHAVIOR When people are being passive, they:	You will usually observe:
- dismiss their own needs as unimportant - devalue themselves—put themselves down - often apologize for what they say, or justify themselves - expect others to guess their wishes - often end up feeling angry with others. Think that the other person should somehow have known what was	- a hesitant, soft or monotone voice - nervous movements, hunched shoulders, downcast eyes - dropping hints about what is happening or what they want—not expressing thoughts, desires, feelings or needs directly - apologizing for what they say, asking permission for their thoughts or actions, frequently justifying themselves

wanted • are about doing nothing and hoping, or trying, to get what they want in a roundabout way	• not confronting people nor attempt to resolve the situation • giving everyone else their choice, putting everyone else first, even at their own expense—'You win, I lose'

The rewards for passive communication include:
- *being taken care of:* having your needs taken care of by someone else
- *being a "nice guy"* that others like because they always get their way
- getting others' *sympathy and support*
- *avoidance of unpleasantness:* avoiding anxiety or responsibilities temporarily, or not having to face fears

However, look at the costs of being passive:
- **loss of control and freedom**—rarely getting one's way
- **distance and destruction of relationships**—due to conflicts never being resolved and resentments increasing
- **low self-esteem**—for not standing up for what you believe is right and giving yourself repeated messages that you are too weak to cope

Think about a relationship where you are having difficulty. Is one of you stuck using passive communication?

While passive people are often giving in and allowing others to control them, they are not **without means of controlling others** as well. **Passive methods of control**—which are not always conscious—include:
- feeling depressed or unmotivated and being a miserable
- refusing to cooperate

- talking behind someone's back
- spreading rumors
- making fun of someone
- not communicating
- withdrawing, evading problems

Do you recognize these aggressive and passive behaviors? Consider how they are impacting on your relationships.

Passive–Aggressive Behavior

One of the difficulties for people who are stuck in passive communication behavior is that they often feel very aggressive but are unable to communicate that openly, so they bottle the feelings up, or display that anger in non-verbal actions. This usually called passive–aggressive behavior.

It makes openness, honesty and trust very difficult in any relationships.

This behavior is often a learned way of protecting ourselves—life experiences that have made this a safe way to be. You will remember some of the key principles from earlier in this book, particularly:
- most people have a reason for their behavior—**which makes sense to them**. You may not see why, but for them it is the best thing—for who they are at that moment
- if what we want is not happening, then we need to **try something different**—to stop doing the same thing over and over again
- what we **do** and what we **are** are two different things—we need to separate the behavior from the person. We are all

more than the behavior we produce—and we can all learn to change our behavior

A good example is where a person has been using passive behavior, expecting the other *"should somehow have known what was wanted"*. As most people are not mind readers, after a while the frustration on the part of the person using passive behavior rises...and they feel angry. But they cannot express their disagreement assertively, so the anger comes out in other ways.

Classic **examples of passive–aggressive behavior** are:
- saying something that is designed for the other person to hear without saying it to them directly
- using sarcasm and put downs, sulking
- using humor to be nasty or hurtful
- pretending to agree to do something, but not doing it, or doing it very slowly
- putting off important tasks for less important ones, and often then apologizing for not getting the job done
- withdrawing love and affection
- making excuses

If you **have identified that many of your behavior patterns involve passive—aggressive communication**, you may be ready to widen your range of options. It is important to do this in a way that feels **safe for you**. Some ideas to try are:
- identify why you feel unable to express negative emotions openly. Get some help to do this, such as a good friend or a counselor
- keep a journal where you can express your negative feelings safely AND identify what positive actions you would like to happen
- prepare an assertive statement. This will help you to step back and understand the behavior, your feelings and what you want to happen

- practice your assertive statement and then use it
- don't give up!

If you find **yourself caught in a passive–aggressive cycle with some one**, it is important to:
- be clear yourself about what is happening
- think about your own role in the cycle—what are you doing or achieving?
- prepare an assertive statement. This will help you to step back and understand the behavior, your feelings and what you want to happen
- practice your assertive statement and then use it
- remember the other assertive techniques—don't get side tracked or caught up in blame

Assertive Behavior

ASSERTIVE BEHAVIOR When people are being Assertive, they:	You will usually observe:
• use a steady, clear and firm voice • match their words and body language	*'I am feeling a little confused, could you go over that again?'*

• make statements which are constructive, free of judgment and blame, for example *'I can make decisions and so can you, we both have the right to an opinion and a choice'* • recognize the rights of other people to have an opinion and to be heard	rather than *'I know I'm so stupid, I just don't understand what you are saying'* or *'You aren't explaining that very well, are you?'* *"You missed the deadline for that report'* rather than *'You're absolutely hopeless at managing your time."*

ASSERTIVE BEHAVIOR When people are being Assertive, they:	**You will usually observe:**
• focus on the behavior not on the person • have discussions in which opinions are expressed-- people can then discuss those, negotiate and then reach a decision, or an outcome, that meets some of the needs of both, or all, of the people involved • are clear and to the point • participate in mutual problem solving in which we strive for ways in	*You seem to be getting complaints from members of the public at the moment. Do you know what the problem is?'* rather than *'You're getting far too many complaints from members of the public recently. What's the matter with you?'*

> which *'we can both win'*

Experience shows that **assertive behavior is a far more effective way** of communicating. It builds your self esteem, demonstrates respect for yourself and others, and changes—and improves—the way you communicate with others.

And like all new skills or habits, it takes some effort...

Here are some examples of various Assertive techniques. Once you have read them, use **Checklist 5** to practice Assertion skills.

Assertiveness techniques

First, when you start to use Assertive Communication there are some things to remember:

- practice—be safe
- know the facts relating to the situation and have the details to hand
- be ready for other people's behavior and prepare your responses
- prepare and use good open questions
- practice your own new reactions to aggressive or passive behavior
- be persistent—trust that if you stick to your process, it will work

Assertive Communication uses a three part statement:
- Behavior—*When you*...what it is, exactly, that the other person has done or is doing
- Feelings—*I feel*...what *feelings* do you experience as a result of their *behavior*?

- **Effect**—*I would like*...what you would like to see happening instead

It is an "I" statement: "When you come late to the meeting—**behavior**—I feel angry because we have to repeat information the rest of us have heard—**feelings**—and I would like you to attend meetings on time—**effect**."

By using this kind of message, you are giving another person complete information, leaving no room for second guessing or doubt. This is much more productive and assertive than simply ignoring the problem or just expressing your anger or frustration.

Look at the examples in the following table:

Technique	Example
The Self Disclosure Statement **Step 1:** **A statement of behavior:** **Identify what is happening— what it is that the other person has done or is doing:** *'When you...............'* **(this should be a statement of facts, as objective as you can be)** **Step 2:** **Identify your feelings as a result of their** *behavior* *'I feel/get/become...'* **(a description of your own feelings or the effect of the action on**	*'When you are late, I feel disappointed, and I would like to work out how we can agree on a time that suits us both.'* or *'When you are late, I often miss my bus, and I would like to work out how we can agree on a time that suits us both.'*

Technique	Example
your feelings) Step 3: Identify what you would like to *happen:* *'I would like……….a description of what you would like without telling the other person what to do*	

Technique	Example
Broken record Use this technique when you are trying to make a point, but the other person seems to be ignoring your request or refusal. Choose a phrase that you feel comfortable with, without getting angry or shouting. Repeat the original assertive statement each time the other person tries to get you to change your mind. Don't be sidetracked. Keep repeating your point, using a low level, pleasant voice. Don't get pulled into arguing or trying to explain yourself. This lets you ignore manipulation, baiting, and irrelevant logic.	*'I can't go with you this evening.'* *'I don't think you heard me, I can't go with you this evening.'* *'This really is not relevant to the issue, which is that I can't go with you this evening'.*

Technique	Example
Saying 'No' It is okay to say 'No'. It is also okay not to feel guilty when you say 'No'. Saying 'No' does not mean that you are rejecting the person—you are simply saying 'No' to this particular request. You can improve the way you say 'No' by using Empathy.	*'No'.* *'I understand that you need to go tonight, but I can't go with you this evening'.*

Technique	Example
Workable Compromise If the Broken Record doesn't work, try and find a compromise that may work for both of you.	*'I can't go with you this evening, but I could go at lunch time tomorrow'.*

Technique	Example
Negative Inquiry Rather that reacting to criticism, try asking for more information about what is prompting the other	Consider how the responses below calm rather than inflame the interaction: 'You are useless at using a street directory!' (inflames) *'What is it about how I use the*

person to make the criticism.	*directory that you don't like?'*(calms)
	'You always give me the directions just before I have to make a turn.'(inflames) *'Would it help if I told you a bit earlier?(calms)* 'Yes, it would'.

As you work through **Checklist 5** you will find that you are in fact improving your emotional competence— your ability to perceive, identify, and manage emotion—as you improve your knowledge of yourself and your understanding of others. It gives us another perspective.

Active Listening

To better understand how and why the listening process can be, at times, so ineffective, you should know that **listening and hearing are not the same.**

Instead, hearing is actually just one stage of listening, which occurs when your ears pick up sound waves and transmit these waves to your brain. On the other hand, listening is a whole communication process.

By understanding the process and utilizing the right tools, you can improve your listening skills, ensuring you do more than hear the words; you actually **comprehend them correctly**.

To receive the communicated message loud and clear, you have to be **an active participant** in the listening process.

Unfortunately, our **thought speed is much faster than our speech speed**, which can prompt your brain to start working ahead of the speaker. Perhaps you are simply considering the speaker's next comments, or the answer to a question you feel certain will come up.

Effective listening can be a challenge as:
- people vary in how clearly they express themselves
- we have different needs and purposes for communicating
- messages are sent and received in different ways

Active listening **with a purpose** is used to gain information, to determine how another person feels, and to understand others.

Effective active listeners:
- spend more time listening than talking
- don't finish the sentence of others
- don't answer questions with questions
- are aware of their biases. We all have them. We need to work around them
- never daydream or become preoccupied with their own thoughts when others talk
- let the other speaker talk. Don't dominate the conversation

Try to plan responses **after the other has finished speaking...NOT while they are speaking**. Keep your full concentration on what they

are saying, not on what you are going to respond with. For example:
- provide feedback but do not interrupt incessantly
- analyze by looking at all the relevant factors and asking open-ended questions
- summarize

Listening can be one of our most powerful communication tools! Be sure to use it!

The **first step, listening** to the words said, requires total concentration. The **second step, paraphrasing**, requires an accurate review of what was heard and verification that it was accurately understood. Learn and practice these skills.

Step 1: Listen carefully to the words

As you listen to the words, look at the person speaking and try to grasp both the content and the meaning of the words. While this may sound simple, you will find that internal and external distractions keep you from focusing on what the person is saying.

Internal distractions are thoughts that develop while someone else is talking. Sometimes they are related to what the person is saying. Other times you may be thinking about the next question you might ask. You must try and stop these internal distractions that keep you from focusing on what is being said.

External distractions are those things happening around you that compete with the speaker. They can be noises outside, from two people whispering, or perhaps a mobile phone ringing. Exclude them, or at least try not to give attention to them, until your person has finished speaking. Alternatively, stop the person speaking until this distraction is eliminated.

Step 2: Paraphrase what was said

Paraphrasing is a **restatement in your own words** of what someone else said. It should accurately review and clarify the original statement. Asking the original speaker for a verification of your accuracy will help you determine how good a listener you are. The value of paraphrasing is that:
- it clarifies what the speaker said
- it is helpful when the speaker rambles
- it is helpful when the speaker gives conflicting or complex information
- it provides a better understanding of what was said

When paraphrasing, start with the words, "I hear you saying…" or "As I understand it…" Ask the person if what you paraphrased was accurate. If it was, you can move on. If it was paraphrased inaccurately or important details were missed, then you can ask the person to repeat the information needed to complete your understanding.

Questioning techniques

There are some different ways of asking questions that can assist in getting the right information.

Open Questions	These usually start with: where, when, how, who, what and why. They designed to get people thinking and to give them an opportunity to give information
Closed Questions	The are designed to get a 'Yes' or 'No' answer, to focus information, or to clarify precise meaning
Reflective Questions	Usually start with a statement like "So, what I understand is that you…" They reflect what the person has said—to confirm understanding and meaning

Good communicators DO:

- greet the person by name
- are polite
- treat each person as an individual
- listen actively

- ask questions to remove ambiguities and obtain facts
- gain the person's confidence
- are helpful and tactful
- remain neutral
- maintain eye contact
- are firm and decisive
- check with some one else when you are not sure

Good communicators Try Not To:

- try not to lose their temper
- try not to lose patience
- try not to lose professional perspective
- try not to forget that they may be representing an organization
- try not to keep people waiting
- try not to interview people out of turn
- try not to guess answers to a person's questions

In the following tables there are some techniques you can use with someone who is angry or upset or just being difficult.

Some More Techniques for Dealing with Difficult Communication Situations

Technique	Comments
Don't take it personally	Understand that most angry people aren't angry with you personally, but rather with the situation in which they currently find themselves. They may be frustrated and, until you hear them out,

Technique	Comments
	you have no idea why. Until you hear them out, they will not be able to hear you
Read the body language	Make sure you are actively listening to both what is being said and what is <u>not</u> being said. A person's body language—including tone of voice—makes up to 90% of the meaning in any conversation, and it is the body language rather than the words that are telling the true story. If someone is saying "that's okay' and the body language is agitated or upset, then the reality is that whatever the conversation is about is <u>not</u> fine. Good communicators look for and respond to the body language

Technique	Comments
Let them vent	Part of being good at communication is letting the person feel that they are being heard. Let them tell you the entire story. Take notes if it is long or involved. Only after the person has felt like they have said their piece should you attempt to deal with the issues. This is then a good time to use Reflective questions

Ask for clarification	Better to ask than to start off on the wrong path. If you begin by answering a question they didn't ask, the person's frustration may intensify. Make sure you know what it is that has happened and perhaps what they want done about it before you begin

Technique	Comments
Validate the person	Work with the person—their feelings are valid for them. It is useful to let the person know that you understand that they may be frustrated or upset—but NOT that you understand how they feel—you don't! This is not admitting fault or accepting blame for the situation. It just further lets the person know that you are there to assist
Use Reflective Questions	To make sure you have understood—and often to clarify for the person just what it is that is happening or they are asking for—use reflective questions. Reflective questions also help to uncover other issues
You don't have to have all the answers	Saying "I don't know, but I will check" is quite appropriate. It is worse to guess or give incorrect information that then has to be changed. Make

	sure you follow up with the person when you said you would!

Technique	Comments
Share your commonalities focusing on the differences	<u>In some circumstances</u>, it may be useful to identify something that you both have in common. Perhaps share a short story about something similar that happened to you. This can help to break down barriers
Tell the person what you can do for them	If you can do exactly what the person wants, great! If you can't, try and offer options. It is also important that you know when to stop, and to refer the person to someone else

Technique	Comments
Ask the person what they would like you to do	Sometimes the person may not even know what they want from you. Reflecting this back—with respect—may help them realize that they are being unreasonable. It is also appropriate to ask a person what they think would work for them—this can often be a good starting point for negotiation
Explain why you may be limited in what you can do	If it simply isn't possible to do what they want, explain that openly and honestly with the person

Be aware—no matter how skilful and careful you are, there are some situations where you are simply not going to get all the information you need, or where nothing you can do or offer will satisfy the person's perceived needs. And nothing you can do defuses the person's anger or dislike.

You may find that you need to **ask for help** with this particular person, or just accept that some encounters will just be difficult. Discuss the situation with colleagues or your manager, and stay calm!

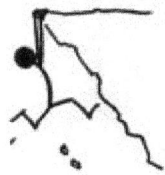

The World of Virtual Interpersonal Communication

There is a **virtual and face to face balance** we need to think about when using SMS, Twitter, email, FaceBook, chat rooms and other social networking tools.

They can be an incredibly quick and convenient way of communicating short messages, but they may not be the best way to communicate for some situations and people.

Almost by their nature, they seem to **encourage an immediate, instinctive and emotional response**, yet we often use them in situations where face to face communication would be far more effective.

When this is combined with our tendency to be very informal in the cyber world, then poor or even disastrous communication can happen.

There are both positives and negatives to using virtual communication tools, which are worth having in the back of your mind when you are deciding how to communicate.

Among the **positives** are that they:
- allow us to keep immediate contact with people both close by and very far away—and at significantly lower cost than in the past
- can allow immediate communication—questions, arrangements and plans
- enable easy and quick sharing of experiences with anyone, such as holiday photos or emergency information
- can enable time to reflect and contemplate
- are part of our information flow rather than requiring total attention – you can text while doing something else and not appear to be ignoring the other person
- give us the opportunity to check on facts or get more information while carrying on the social media conversation
- may give us a record of what was said, by whom and to whom, and when

We are still learning about some of the **negatives**, but so far they appear to be that:
- humor, sarcasm and irony don't come across well—even if you use ☺ or ☹
- while it may seem easier or safer to apologize for some action using SMS, it rarely has successful or lasting outcomes—face to face is better. The same goes for most kinds of bad news!
- there is some evidence relationships can suffer if there is too much virtual communication and too little face to face communication
- virtual communication may tend to be more one dimensional, partly because there is no body language to improve understanding of interpersonal cues
- digital conflict resolution is rarely very effective
- they can often be poor ways of attempting to have meaningful conversations

- too much texting and too little writing can lead to poor business writing skills, particularly in being able to adapt writing style to match the needs of the audience
- there can be blurring of the boundaries between public and private. This is both in terms of when people may be contacted, e.g. via SMS or text at anytime of the day or night, or what can be put into the public domain, e.g. information put onto a personal FaceBook page or comments on Twitter
- whatever you say may end up anywhere, with anyone and at anytime now or in the future
- it is very easy to lie in the cyber world! And equally hard to find out when someone is lying…

Some Simple Rules

Rule 1: Think before you go virtual

Is this the best way to have this conversation?

Would it be better—even if a little more uncomfortable—to actually talk to this person face to face?

Would I like to receive this communication virtually? Or would I prefer it face to face? Why?

Have you provided opportunities for people to ask questions?

Have you considered how formal or informal you need to be in this communication? Do you need to use a hard copy?

Rule 2: Think before you reply

If some virtual communication has upset you, made you angry or simply annoyed you, then certainly draft your answer. **But don't send it yet.**

Remember—we tend to lose the emotional filters we generally apply in face to face communication as soon as we go virtual.

Follow these steps:

1. GET UP, WALK AWAY for at least 5 minutes, then, re–read what you've written.

2. Ask yourself: '*What would be the impact if I said what I have written in this SMS, FaceBook entry, chat room, email, etc to the addressee in person?*"

3. If the answer is that you wouldn't say it, or it may make the situation worse—then rethink it, and consider not sending it. Try something different!

'You cannot shake hands with a clenched fist.'
Mahatma Gandhi

Collaborative problem resolution

There are times when we all differ with the ideas, priorities, or statements of others—that is human nature! It is a good way for us to clarify and improve our own ideas. **Difference is especially valuable** because it often leads to new and better ways of doing things, and enables us to learn.

Good communicators learn to manage conflict effectively.

We can experience difficulties in our dealings with people for many reasons. Some common ones are:
- **miscommunication**: not listening well to each other, or misunderstanding what is said and what is meant
- **confusion**: where goals or roles are not defined, or processes and procedures are not working—or workable
- **differences in preferences**: the ways in which we see and describe the world
- **personal needs**: when our everyday personal needs or interests are threatened

There are many ways of handling differences, depending on issues such as:
- the culture of the family, group, organization and community
- the skills of the people involved
- the communication styles of the people involved—their preferences

Disagreements, differences or conflict can be healthy or they can be destructive—it all depends on how they are addressed.

One of the key factors in how we address them is how our culture deals with them.

For some cultures, harmony and consensus are central; in others, individuality and independence are valued; while for yet others, the heritage and pride of the group, and loyalty to the leader are the highest priority.

Some people avoid conflict, others confront, while still others try to compromise or collaborate. **Collaboration is the most productive way of resolving differences—it may take a little longer but it has lasting results.**

The first steps in dealing with difficulties and disagreements are:
- **stop** talking
- **listen** carefully
- **clarify** meanings
- find out what the other person is **feeling**
- consider **behavior** preferences
- **summarize** and reflect back what is being said
- **look for common ground**
- **avoid** demanding, criticizing and defending language

- use **non-threatening, non-judgmental** language

Work together more collaboratively. Use:
Checklist 6—Disagreements, differences and conflict

Conclusion

It *is* hard work—but perhaps some of the most *rewarding* hard work there can be!

Please remember to keep using your Checklists as you move along on your communication journey.

You might also want to file your working copies of **Checklist 1— Changing Habits** and **Checklist 5—Practicing Assertion.** Then, bring them out every three or six months, and reflect on how far you have come—and where else you might like to go...

May your journey be peaceful and exhilarating

PostScript. I recently heard a talk by the Dalai Lama, and he said something that resonated with me: be warm hearted—to others and to yourself.

Some useful references

Smith, M. J. 1975, *When I say no, I feel guilty, Bantam*, Canada.
(Still in print and as fresh and relevant as when it was first published!)

Ruiz, Don Miguel 1997, *The four agreements*, Amber–Allen, California.

Riso, Don Richard 1987, *Personality types*, Harper Collins, London.

O'Connor, J. & Seymour, J. 2002, *Introducing NLP,* Harper Collins, London

Dowrick, S. 2000, *The universal heart*, Viking, Victoria.

DeBoard, Robert 1998, *Counselling for toads*, Routledge, London.

Cornelius, H. & Faire, S. 1996, *Everyone can win*, Simon & Schuster, NSW.

Bandler, R. 1985, *Using your brain for a change*, Real People Press, Utah.

Checklist 1—Changing habits: Setting Goals

As you write your Goals, make sure they are:
- Specific; Measurable; Achievable; Relevant; Time bound
- **SMALL**—make them manageable, both in terms of time and what you are going to do
- **SPECIFIC**—goals need to be definite and detailed, something you can see yourself doing
- **REASONABLE**—each goal should make sense, you should be able to see the value in doing it
- **POSITIVE**—decide what you will do rather than what you will not do
- **REPETITIOUS**—choose goal behaviour you will be able to work at often
- **INDEPENDENT**—try to set goals that are not dependent on the behaviour of others

Step 1

Prepare yourself a sheet of paper or spreadsheet that has 3 columns:

1. Actions	2. Steps and Resources	3. How will know I have succeeded?

Step 2

Under Column 1—**Actions**—write your answers to these questions:
- What are my goals?
- What will be different?

- What outcomes do I want?
- What do I want to change?

Now fill in the answers to those questions in **Columns 2 and 3**.

Step 3

In a new row in Column 1—write your answers to these questions:

- Who and what will help me achieve my goals?
- What are the possible barriers to success? How might I handle them?

Now fill in the answers to those questions in **Columns 2 and 3**.

Step 4

In a new row in Column 1—write your answers to these questions:
- Who do I need to talk to?
- Who can support me?

Now fill in the answers to those questions in **Columns 2 and 3**.

An Example of a Plan

Scenario:

Jo works with Lee. They have a range of tasks, one of which is to prepare some materials each morning. They are supposed to take turns—Jo doing it one day and Lee the next. However, Lee has not been doing his share—he comes in late at least 4 mornings a week. Jo has been doing the task most mornings.
Jo's tried to talk to Lee about it, but Lee just gets angry and refuses to talk about it. Jo has had it! He wants Lee to do his job properly

and he's sick of the unpleasant atmosphere. Jo decides to try a new approach, using an Assertive technique.
Jane is a work colleague who Jo feels safe to talk with about the issue, and who he's sure will help him practice.

Here is Jo's plan.

1. Actions	2. Steps and Resources	3. How will know I have succeeded?
Goal: Have Lee do his fair share of preparing materials, by the end of next week **Different:** Lee does his turn with no arguing **Change:** Lee takes his turns in preparation, without argument	1. Keep records over a week, so you have evidence of the situation 2. Practice an Assertive statement *"Lee, when you don't take your turn, I feel disappointed and I would like us to agree how we can sort that out"* 3. Find a good time to talk with Lee 4. Talk with Lee	I have spoken with Lee and we have clarified the situation By the end of next week, we are both doing a fair share of preparing the materials, peacefully

1. Actions	2. Steps and Resources	3. How will know I have

		succeeded?
Help: Ask my colleague Jane to help me practice my Assertive statement **Barriers:** Me feeling angry; Lee getting angry; not having a private place to talk to Lee	1. Find time to practice before the end of next week 2. Choose meeting time & place with Lee carefully 3. Try and find out why Lee is being late—maybe that is part of the problem. Have a second Assertive statement ready—maybe **Negative Enquiry** *"Lee, what is it that is causing you to be late and not able to take your turn?*	Lee is listening and we are getting somewhere I have tried to find a Workable Compromise!

1. Actions	2. Steps and Resources	3. How will know I have succeeded?
I need to talk to Jane	Set time up	I feel confident that I can approach Lee

| Think about what I need to say to the other people in our team | Decide who I will talk to and what I will say. Time: after Lee and I have sorted out the situation | People who need to know understand the process Lee and I have been through |

Checklist 2—Planning your Communication

1. **Why are you communicating?**

   - What results do you want?
   - What do you want your audience to know or do as a result of your communication?

2. **Who is your audience?**

   - What are their needs and issues?
   - Have there been changes in your audience?

3. **How will you communicate?**

   - What ways or forms of communication are available?
   - What means of communication does your audience use and respond to? How can you work with the means they use?

4. **What about non verbals—body language—and filters?**

   - What are some possible communication filters—yours and your audience?
   - How will you observe and check body language?

5. **Get Feedback**

    - How will you know that the information has been received and understood?

Checklist 3— Visual Auditory Kinesthetic

Good communicators work to understand their own preferences and those of others, and are able to adapt their interactions to deal with them.

This tool will increase your capacity to understand others from their viewpoint rather than as you see the world.

1. Think about how you interact with others. Who do you communicate **well** with?

2. What is it about the way you communicate that **makes it work well**? For example: is it that we respect each other, or we match VAK styles, or we often check that we have a common understanding, or we use assertive techniques, or something else?

3. Now ask yourself the same questions about people with whom **you don't communicate quite so well**. What is it that is happening?

4. Are there **any patterns** in both your good communication situations and in your not so good situations? What works and what doesn't?

5. What have you learned from this tool that might give you some insight to what works well and not so well? **What might you do differently?** With whom? When?

Checklist 4—Practicing Assertion

The key to improving your skills in Assertion is to **plan and practice**, until your responses become part of your usual range of options. This takes some planning and practice—but it does work!

You might like to refer to the examples in the 'Assertive Techniques' pages as you use this Checklist.

1. Identify some times when your interactions with a person—or several people—have
   often been passive or aggressive. What are some of the words that you both use?

2. How would you like to change this—assertively? What would the interaction look
   feel and sound like?

3. Try out a **'Self Disclosure' Statement**.

   When you...

   I feel/get/become...

   and I would like...

4. Can you try **'Broken Record'**?

5. What about **'Saying No'**?

6. Can you try **'Negative Inquiry'**?

Now, practice the response you have chosen, then try it out the next time the situation—or a similar one—occurs. Reflect on how what worked, what didn't, and what you can do better next time. Try watching how others behave, and—to observe yourself—practice how you would deal assertively with the same situation. Use every opportunity you can to prepare yourself to respond assertively.

Checklist 5—Understanding your audience

1. Who are they? What do they know? What are their attitudes?

2. What do they know about you? Have they heard from you before? What has worked in the past and why?

3. Have there been any changes in your audience, leadership or environment? How does your audience communicate now? Can you build on that?

4. Who needs to know what's happening? Who needs to do—or know—something as a result of this communication? Who will be affected by this communication? How much or how little do they need to know?

5. Does your audience need background information?

6. Do they need a computer, special equipment or software? Do they have any special language or access requirements? What impact might the message have on them? How might it change their needs?

7. Who else might be able to assist me in being clear about my audience?

8. How appropriate is it to communicate virtually?

Checklist 6—Disagreements, differences and conflict

You can use this Checklist as a guide to resolving interpersonal issues. Remember to practice your Assertion techniques throughout the process.

Step 1:
- Decide—are we really willing to resolve the conflict?
- If the answer is yes, then agree on how you will proceed—are you both willing to work with this model? Is there another model that we both might agree to use?
- Can we do it by ourselves, or do we need an impartial facilitator?
- Where and when are we going to meet?
- Agree how you will speak—will you each take it in turns to talk, will there be a time limit, will you summarize what you have understood?

Step 2:
- Clarify the problem or issue—clearly state what you each understand as the issue
- Address the issue, not the person
- Look for common areas—these may be common goals, frustrations, needs

Step 3:
- Brainstorm some possible options—think creatively and identify a range of possible options. Try not to evaluate at this point

- Once you have a range of options, now evaluate possibilities. If all these options are discounted, revisit the problem or issue to make sure you are clear on it, then try brainstorming some more options

Step 4:
- Decide together on the best possible option
- If there are several possibilities, prioritize them separately, then share your priorities and find out whether there is one that you can both accept

Step 5:
- Agree on how you will put the option into place—what is your Action Plan?
- Decide who will do what, when, how, how often and by when

Step 6:
- Plan how you will evaluate the solution
- What will you do if the option does not work?
- Identify how you will evaluate what have you learned as a result of this process?

Disclaimer

We have used our best efforts in preparing this material, and in ensuring that it is free from errors and omissions.

However, we do not accept responsibility for injury loss or damage occasioned to any person acting, or refraining from action, as a result of this material.

Author Profile

J H Hood has a Bachelor of Arts, a Diploma in Education and the National Medal. She has extensive experience across government, the private sector and community organizations: as a senior manager as well as training adults in the workplace in a wide range of management and personal skills.

She has worked with many thousands of people, helping them to build the skills to survive and thrive in the workplace. Feedback on her training and coaching focuses on how practical her material is, and how quickly positive outcomes come from using it.

The 'How To" series comes form her love of writing and her experience helping people build their skills and knowledge.

She and her partner live in the foothills of Adelaide, South Australia, where they can watch koalas climbing the trees outside her study window. Their two cats don't even stir!

The delightful graphics are by Mal Briggs, Canberra.

How to Book of Meetings: Conducting Effective Meetings

Have you just been asked to chair a meeting, or take the minutes, or set up a meeting agenda? Need some help? Would samples of an agenda or minutes be useful? What about some techniques for chairing a meeting or dealing with difficult people? Then this 60 page "How to" book is for you.

"How to Book of Writing Skills: Words at Work"

Enhance and Improve Your English Skills: Learn How to Write Emails, Reports, Documents and More

Have you ever been frustrated by your boss constantly making changes to your documents? Annoyed at the time it takes to write something? Sick of sending emails that don't get read? Been asked to write a report and don't know where to start? Are people just not getting your message? Then this guide is for you!

In this 90 page guide you will find practical and proven techniques to write clearly, concisely and quickly.

Look out for more eBooks in the" How to" Series...coming soon.

www.ingramcontent.com/pod-product-compliance
Lightning Source LLC
Chambersburg PA
CBHW071412040426
42444CB00009B/2208